Sounding the Seasons

Sounding the Seasons

*Seventy Sonnets
for the Christian Year*

Malcolm Guite

CANTERBURY
PRESS

Norwich

© Malcolm Guite 2012

First published in 2012 by the Canterbury Press Norwich
Editorial office
3rd Floor, Invicta House,
108–114 Golden Lane,
London EC1Y OTG.

Ninth impression February 2019

Canterbury Press is an imprint of Hymns Ancient & Modern Ltd
(a registered charity)
13A Hellesdon Park Road, Norwich,
Norfolk, NR6 5DR, UK

www.canterburypress.co.uk

British Library Cataloguing in Publication data

A catalogue record for this book is available
from the British Library

978 1 84825 274 5

Typeset by Manila Typesetting Company
Printed and bound in Great Britain by
CPI Group (UK) Ltd, Croydon

Contents

CONTENTS

To the glory of God
and for the Household of Faith
at St Edward King and Martyr, Cambridge,
among whom these sonnets first lived and breathed.

After this the Lord appointed seventy
others and sent them on ahead of
him in pairs to every town and
place where he himself
intended to go.
Luke 10.1

Introduction

This book offers the reader a cycle of 70 sonnets, running in sequence from Advent, at the beginning of the Church year, to the feast of Christ the King at its end.

I was conscious as I composed this sequence of the longer traditions, both ecclesiastical and literary, in which I worked. Within those traditions, two great poetry sequences stand out, to both of which I am indebted for inspiration and example.

The first is George Herbert's *The Temple*,[1] which was published posthumously by Herbert's friend Nicholas Ferrar in 1633 and has been in print ever since. *The Temple* stands not only as a beautiful monument in literature but also, as its author intended, as a gateway, a 'church porch', through which many have entered, to walk across 'the church floor', to be lit by the 'windowes', to come to the altar, to the table where Love bids us welcome. For *The Temple* Herbert made use not only of the sonnet, but also of many other forms of his own finding and invention. His double vocation as priest and poet continues to be an inspiration, and if, nearly four hundred years later, I can help with these sonnets to furnish some small part of that Temple whose doors he has opened to the world, I will be more than content.

It was some two hundred years later, and a little under two hundred years ago, that the second sequence to which I have

---

[1] For a good text see George Herbert, *The Complete English Works*, edited and introduced by Ann Pasternak Slater (London: Everyman, 1995).

alluded was published. In 1827 John Keble brought out *The Christian Year*,[2] a book in which each poem took as its point of departure one of the Sundays of the liturgical year, and drew for its thought and imagery on the lectionary readings provided for that day in the Book of Common Prayer. Keble's wonderful book kindled the imagination and inspired the devotion of many Christians throughout the nineteenth century, and in that century alone it went through more than a hundred editions. Some of Keble's poems, such as 'New Every Morning is the Love', also found their way into the canon of popular hymns, which is where they really flourish now. Again I am indebted to Keble, as to Herbert, for the inspiration in making this little book. Whereas Herbert had organized his poems according to the shape and layout of the church as sacred space, mapping as it were a journey from the church porch via the font to the altar and the sacrament of communion, Keble made his poems staging posts on a journey through sacred time, marking and deepening the transitions and crossing places that make the sacral year.

For *Sounding the Seasons* I have followed Keble's example of a journey through time, but whereas he made a poem for each Sunday of the year, whether it fell on a great feast day or not, I have responded instead to the feeling that liturgical time is not quite the same as chronological time. It is not regular and evenly spaced. Some times and seasons are richer and deeper than others, more intricately layered. The great turning points, Advent and Christmas, Lent, Holy Week and Easter, seemed to me to call for more than many of the individual Sundays in the longer seasons. In order to 'sound the seasons' in every sense, I felt the need for some particular and concentrated sonnet sequences within the larger cycle to register the greater depth of these special times, times when *Kairos* enters, opens and breaks into *Chronos*. So I have special sequences for

---

[2] Sadly this book is no longer in print but is widely available on the internet and as an ebook, for example at: http://www.gutenberg.org/ebooks/4272

Advent, Christmastide, Epiphany, Lent and Holy Week, and at the heart of the book a 'double corona' sequence on the Stations of the Cross for Good Friday and Easter Sunday.

The mention of the term 'double corona' brings me to acknowledge a third debt of gratitude to a great figure in the tradition. John Donne[3] is the other poet-priest who continues to be a personal and literary inspiration. His *Holy Sonnets*, and in particular his sequence of seven sonnets called 'La Corona', have served as an example and encouragement in this endeavour. Donne's clarity and honesty, his willingness to press the depth and complexity, the paradoxes and contradictions of our experience of faith, drew him to the sonnet as the form whose discipline, brevity and concentrated 'muscle' perfectly suited his special fusion of thought and feeling. In 'La Corona', Donne wrote a cycle of seven sonnets, linked into a 'corona' or crown, touching on the mysteries of the major festivals of the year, from the Annunciation to the Ascension, in which the interlinking line shared by each successive sonnet suggested the essential unity of all those separate aspects of faith that we choose to celebrate on different days. I followed his example, using linked lines in a modified form in the fifteen sonnets of my 'Stations of the Cross'.

The Sonnet and the Sonnet Sequence

Mention of Donne's extraordinary achievement leads me to say something briefly about the sonnet as a form, and about the sonnet sequence as both a tradition and a larger form in itself.

The sonnet, which had its origins in Italian poetry in the thirteenth century, has proved a wonderfully flexible and delicate instrument in the hands of writers in English over the course of many centuries. At the heart of its virtues are brevity, clarity, concentration, and a capacity for paradox, for expressing,

---

[3] See *The Poems of John Donne*, edited by Herbert Grierson (Oxford: Oxford University Press, 1949).

juxtaposing and containing contradiction, all of which are required if we are to approach the paradox and mystery that is at the heart of the Christian faith.

Don Paterson, the Scottish poet who is one of the modern masters of the sonnet form, has written brilliantly about the constraints and powers of this form in the Introduction to his anthology *101 Sonnets*:

> As poetry moved slowly off the tongue and onto the page, the visual appeal of an approximately square field of black text on a sheet of white paper must have been impossible to resist. Which is what the sonnet is, first and foremost: a small square poem. It presents both poet and reader with a vivid symmetry that is the perfect emblem of the meaning a sonnet seeks to embody . . . so a sonnet is a paradox, a little squared circle, a mandala that invites our meditation.[4]

He also points out that even with the immense variety of stanza breaks and rhyme schemes available within the sonnet itself, the 'turn' or 'volta' at about line 8 – between the octet and the sestet of the classic 'Petrarchan' sonnet – is a feature even of those sonnets that do not formally break down into an 8 and a 6. So in the English or 'Shakespearian' form of the sonnet, in which the fourteen lines are arranged in three quatrains and a couplet, it is nevertheless true that a 'turn' or change in feel or mood, a new stage or development in thought and feeling, often occurs at or around line 8. Patterson thinks this is a reflection of the rule of the golden section, a just proportion, whose implications he explores at some length.

In this sequence I have for the most part followed the 'Shakespearian' form but have also included, where appropriate, some Petrarchan sonnets and some other variations of my own invention.

---

[4] *101 Sonnets from Shakespeare to Heaney*, edited by Don Paterson (London: Faber & Faber, 1999), p. xiii.

I am also interested in poetry as it sounds 'on the tongue' as well as how it looks 'on the page', and it seems to me that one of the attractions of the sonnet form for use in prayer and liturgy is that it can be spoken and heard in almost exactly one minute, a period of time in which we can achieve complete concentration, anticipation and recall of what we have heard. So a sonnet is indeed, as Dante Gabriel Rosetti memorably called it, 'a moment's monument', and I have alluded to that in the prologue or opening sonnet of my sequence.

Another immense advantage of the sonnet as a form through which to explore the meaning and resonance of the Christian faith, and through which to praise and celebrate a God whose beauty is 'always ancient, always new', is that the sonnet itself is always ancient, always new. On the one hand it has a long history, and simply as a form in itself summons the memory and achievement of great writers of the past; on the other it has been constantly renewed and reinvented in every generation. There is a danger of pastiche and archaism for anyone who chooses to take up the sonnet as a form, but the sonnet itself is always capable of speaking in a contemporary voice. In seeking for ways in which the sonnet can speak with that contemporary voice while still summoning and retaining the music and resonance inherent in its form, I have had before me the examples of three great living poets who have made this instrument their own.

Geoffrey Hill proved himself a complete master of this form in the sequence of seven sonnets called 'Lachrymae' in his book *Tenebrae*,[5] and it was reading that when it came out in 1978 that persuaded me that the sonnet could be used without pastiche or archaism to address issues that were at once ancient and contemporary. Seamus Heaney has used both individual sonnets and short sequences throughout his work in ways that still continue to astonish and delight, and his beautiful

---

[5] Geoffrey Hill, *Tenebrae* (London: André Deutsch, 1978).

sequence 'Glanmore Sonnets' in *Field Work*[6] has been a continuous inspiration to me as an example of the sheer musicality of language concentrated into fourteen lines in the hands of a master. Finally, *Orpheus*,[7] Don Paterson's wonderful 'version' of Rainer Maria Rilke's *Sonnets to Orpheus*, has provided me with an example of a longer contemporary sonnet sequence in which the language and cadence have been capable of expressing both the complexity and the mystery of our being here.

The sonnet sequence, or cycle, can also be regarded as a 'form' or at any rate a genre in itself. There are a number of famous sonnet sequences in which, while each poem can still be read individually, the whole sequence works on a larger scale – it tells a story and can be seen in some lights as a single long poem broken down into a series of fourteen-line stanzas. Spenser's *Amoretti*, Shakespeare's *Sonnets*, and Elizabeth Barrett Browning's *Sonnets from the Portuguese* are all examples of sequences from which we can draw individual poems but which, taken together, develop distinct themes and tell a larger story. I have been conscious of this long tradition in making this sequence, which I hope can also be read as a single poem with various threads of connection and development between its stanzas. I enjoy the Elizabethan playfulness with numerology and sonnet numbering, but have not indulged in it myself, except in my choice of the total number of sonnets in the sequence.

Some ways to use this book

This discussion of the ways in which sonnet sequences can be read both as collections of individual poems and as a single work leads me to some final comments about the ways in which this book might be read and used.

---

[6] Seamus Heaney, *Field Work* (London: Faber & Faber, 1979).

[7] Don Paterson, *Orpheus: A Version of Rilke's* Die Sonette an Orpheus (London: Faber & Faber, 2006).

I certainly hope it can be read for pleasure as a single sequence, possibly in a single sitting, and for that reason all the sonnets themselves are printed together in sequence, without interruption or any other material or explanation between them. Considered as a single sequence, the whole cycle is a journey through time from Earth to Heaven, so it begins in time with an earthly echo of the heavenly 'Sanctus' and ends with a glimpse of the thrice-holy 'Sanctus, Sanctus, Sanctus', which joins the worship of Earth and Heaven.

The book can also be used, quite properly, as a quarry for the smaller sequences and individual poems it contains. To help with this approach, the smaller sets or sequences – for Advent, Epiphany and so forth – have been numbered and titled appropriately so that readers can extract them from the larger sequence and read them on their own.

Then of course the larger sequence 'sounds the seasons' and makes a journey through the year, and can in that sense be read seasonally and slowly through the year. This may well be the way churches or church groups would like to use this book, especially those who would like to set the poems into liturgy or as readings. Here the sonnet form itself is especially helpful as it obliges anyone who reads it out loud to pay serious attention to the sound and music inherent in the meter and rhyme schemes, so that the language is itself a pleasure to hear. A sonnet is also brief enough to take in at one sitting, but as a form it encourages the kind of compression and concentration that repays rereading.

These poems grew organically out of my own experience of the life and worship of the church of St Edward King and Martyr in Cambridge. They began as a small set of seven sonnets for Advent, written in response to the seven ancient Latin Advent Antiphons, which in their time had contributed so much to the making of the Advent hymn 'O come, O come, Emmanuel'. I found that these seven sonnets struck a chord with many who were seeking to recover Advent as a season of penitence and preparation, and were interested more generally in rediscovering the Church's traditional times and seasons. The sonnets worked well in a liturgical setting and so I was encouraged to continue writing these brief reflective verses that might both articulate our inner response to the times and seasons of the year and also form a resource that could enrich and vary the liturgy and readings of the Church. Just as the Advent poems were written in response to an ancient text already given, the 'Great O' Antiphons,[8] so all the subsequent poems have been written in response to the 'given' texts and feast days that we all share through a common lectionary.

I am also conscious that this book might be a useful resource for clergy, worship leaders and preachers looking for extra material to go with particular festivals, seasons or readings. My colleague at St Edwards, Canon Fraser Watts, has written an essay setting out a little of the history and principles of the liturgical use of 'non-scriptural' readings, together with an account of how he himself has made liturgical use of some of these sonnets. This can be found in Appendix B. A further aid in setting these poems within a coherent service can be found in the two indexes at the end of this book; a Scriptural Index, which allows you to look up a biblical passage and see if there is a poem in this sequence related to it, and a Seasonal Index, which allows you to look up feast days and saints' days and see which poems might be relevant on each particular day.

Since the days of the Romantic poets, and perhaps even more so among the 'post moderns', English poetry has taken an 'inward' turn. It has been seen as the private lyric utterance, sometimes tormented and confessional, of a particular individual, rather than as the public expression or celebration of truths and mysteries to which everyone has access. There is of course a place for the inward, the private and the obscure, in literature as in life, but it seemed to me good to try to recover, in my own small way, what was once a great tradition of more public and accessible poetry.

---

[8] For the texts of these antiphons, see Appendix A.

Acknowledgements

Acknowledgements are due to the editors of the following publications, in which some of these poems have appeared:

The Church Times, *Christianity and Literature*, *The Best Spiritual Writing 2013*, *Seen*, *Radix*, *The Temenos Academy Review*, and *Sehnsucht: The C. S. Lewis Journal*.

A version of some of these sonnets also appears on Steve Bell's CD, *Keening For The Dawn*.

These sonnets took shape in the midst of my life and work as a priest at the church of St Edward King and Martyr in Cambridge. The support, interest and engagement of that household of faith, with whom these sonnets have been shared over the last few years, has been invaluable. I am especially grateful to Canon Fraser Watts, the Vicar-Chaplain and liturgist of that community, both for his support as a fellow priest and for the helpful essay on the liturgical use of these sonnets, which is to be found in Appendix B.

In writing these sonnets I have had the support and encouragement of my colleagues at Girton College, my friends and family and, as publication drew near, I have been especially grateful to Dr Holly Ordway and Dr Michael Ward, who have given me the benefit of their wisdom and discernment as readers and critics, and their insights as creative writers. They have helped me with the sequencing and numbering of these sonnets, as well as with a number of textual emendations. Dr Ordway has also offered me vital assistance in composing the liturgical and scriptural indexes at the back of this book.

THE SONNETS

Prologue: Sounding the seasons

Tangled in time, we go by hints and guesses,
Turning the wheel of each returning year.
But in the midst of failures and successes
We sometimes glimpse the love that casts out fear.
Sometimes the heart remembers its own reasons
And beats a *Sanctus* as we sing our story,
Tracing the threads of grace, sounding the seasons
That lead at last through time to timeless glory.
From the first yearning for a Saviour's birth
To the full joy of knowing sins forgiven,
We start our journey here on God's good earth
To catch an echo of the choirs of heaven.
I send these out, returning what was lent,
Turning to praise each 'moment's monument'.

The lectern

Some rise on eagles' wings, this one is plain,
Plain English workmanship in solid oak.
Age gracefully, it says, *go with the grain.*
You walk towards an always open book,
Open as every life to every light,
Open to shade and shadow, day and night,
The changeless witness of your changing pain.
Be still, the lectern says, *stand here and read.*
Here are your mysteries, your love and fear,
And, running through them all, the slender thread
Of God's strange grace, red as these ribbons, red
As your own blood when reading reads you here
And pierces joint and marrow . . . So you stand,
The lectern still beneath your trembling hand.

THE FOUR EVANGELISTS

Matthew

First of the four, Saint Matthew is the Man;
A Gospel that begins with generation,
Family lines entwine around the Son
Born in Judea, born for every nation,
Born under Law that all the Law of Moses
Might be fulfilled and flower into Grace;
A hidden thread of words and deeds discloses
Eternal love within a human face.
This is the Gospel of the great reversal:
A wayside weed is Solomon in glory,
The smallest sparrow's fall is universal
And Christ is the heart of every human story:
'I will be with you, though you may not see,
And all you do, you do it unto me.'

Mark

A wingèd lion, swift, immediate,
Mark is the Gospel of the sudden shift
From first to last, from grand to intimate,
From strength to weakness, and from debt to gift,
From a wide desert's haunted emptiness
To a close city's fervid atmosphere,
From a voice crying in the wilderness
To angels in an empty sepulchre.
And Christ makes the most sudden shift of all;
From swift action as a strong Messiah,
Casting the very demons back to hell,
To slow pain, and death as a pariah.
We see our Saviour's life and death unmade
And flee his tomb dumbfounded and afraid.

Luke

His Gospel is itself a living creature,
A ground and glory round the throne of God,
Where earth and heaven breathe through human nature
And One upon the throne sees it is good.
Luke is the living pillar of our healing,
A lowly ox, the servant of the four,
We turn his page to find his face revealing
The wonder and the welcome of the poor.
He breathes good news to all who bear a burden,
Good news to all who turn and try again,
The meek rejoice and prodigals find pardon,
A lost thief reaches paradise through pain,
The voiceless find their voice in every word
And, with our Lady, magnify our Lord.

John

This is the Gospel of the primal light,
The first beginning, and the fruitful end,
The soaring glory of an eagle's flight,
The quiet touch of a beloved friend.
This is the Gospel of our transformation,
Water to wine and grain to living bread,
Blindness to sight and sorrow to elation,
And Lazarus himself back from the dead!
This is the Gospel of all inner meaning,
The heart of heaven opened to the earth,
A gentle friend on Jesus' bosom leaning,
And Nicodemus offered a new birth.
No need to search the heavens high above,
Come close with John, and feel the pulse of Love.

THE GREAT O ANTIPHONS

O Sapientia

I cannot think unless I have been thought,
Nor can I speak unless I have been spoken;
I cannot teach except as I am taught,
Or break the bread except as I am broken.
O Mind behind the mind through which I seek,
O Light within the light by which I see,
O Word beneath the words with which I speak,
O founding, unfound Wisdom, finding me,
O sounding Song whose depth is sounding me,
O Memory of time, reminding me,
My Ground of Being, always grounding me,
My Maker's bounding line, defining me:
Come, hidden Wisdom, come with all you bring,
Come to me now, disguised as everything.

O Adonai

Unsayable, you chose to speak one tongue;
Unseeable, you gave yourself away;
The Adonai, the Tetragrammaton,
Grew by a wayside in the light of day.
O you who dared to be a tribal God,
To own a language, people and a place,
Who chose to be exploited and betrayed,
If so you might be met with face to face:
Come to us here, who would not find you there,
Who chose to know the skin and not the pith,
Who heard no more than thunder in the air,
Who marked the mere events and not the myth;
Touch the bare branches of our unbelief
And blaze again like fire in every leaf.

O Radix

All of us sprung from one deep-hidden seed,
Rose from a root invisible to all.
We knew the virtues once of every weed,
But, severed from the roots of ritual,
We surf the surface of a wide-screen world
And find no virtue in the virtual.
We shrivel on the edges of a wood
Whose heart we once inhabited in love,
Now we have need of you, forgotten Root,
The stock and stem of every living thing
Whom once we worshipped in the sacred grove,
For now is winter, now is withering
Unless we let you root us deep within,
Under the ground of being, graft us in.

O Clavis

Even in the darkness where I sit
And huddle in the midst of misery
I can remember freedom, but forget
That every lock must answer to a key,
That each dark clasp, sharp and intimate,
Must find a counter-clasp to meet its guard.
Particular, exact and intricate,
The clutch and catch that meshes with its ward.
I cry out for the key I threw away
That turned and over turned with certain touch
And with the lovely lifting of a latch
Opened my darkness to the light of day.
O come again, come quickly, set me free,
Cut to the quick to fit, the master key.

O Oriens

First light and then first lines along the east
To touch and brush a sheen of light on water,
As though behind the sky itself they traced
The shift and shimmer of another river
Flowing unbidden from its hidden source;
The Day-Spring, the eternal Prima Vera.
Blake saw it too. Dante and Beatrice
Are bathing in it now, away upstream . . .
So every trace of light begins a grace
In me, a beckoning. The smallest gleam
Is somehow a beginning and a calling:
'Sleeper awake, the darkness was a dream
For you will see the Dayspring at your waking,
Beyond your long last line the dawn is breaking.'

O Rex Gentium

O King of our desire whom we despise,
King of the nations never on the throne,
Unfound foundation, cast-off cornerstone,
Rejected joiner, making many one:
You have no form or beauty for our eyes,
A King who comes to give away his crown,
A King within our rags of flesh and bone.
We pierce the flesh that pierces our disguise,
For we ourselves are found in you alone.
Come to us now and find in us your throne,
O King within the child within the clay,
O hidden King who shapes us in the play
Of all creation. Shape us for the day
Your coming Kingdom comes into its own.

O Emmanuel

O come, O come, and be our God-with-us,
O long-sought with-ness for a world without,
O secret seed, O hidden spring of light.
Come to us Wisdom, come unspoken Name,
Come Root, and Key, and King, and holy Flame,
O quickened little wick so tightly curled,
Be folded with us into time and place,
Unfold for us the mystery of grace
And make a womb of all this wounded world.
O heart of heaven beating in the earth,
O tiny hope within our hopelessness,
Come to be born, to bear us to our birth,
To touch a dying world with new-made hands
And make these rags of time our swaddling bands.

CHRISTMASTIDE

1 Mary

You bore for me the One who came to bless
And bear for all, to make the broken whole.
You heard his call, and in your open 'yes'
You spoke aloud for every living soul.
Oh gracious Lady, child of your own child,
Whose mother-love still calls the child in me,
Call me again, for I am lost and wild
Waves surround me now. On this dark sea
Shine as a star and call me to the shore.
Open a door that all my sins would close
And hold me in your garden. Let me share
The prayer that folds the petals of the Rose.
Enfold me too in love's last mystery,
And bring me to the One you bore for me.

2 On the edge

Christmas sets the centre on the edge;
The edge of town, out-buildings of an inn,
The fringe of empire, far from privilege
And power, on the edge and outer spin
Of turning worlds, a margin of small stars
That edge a galaxy itself light years
From some unguessed-at cosmic origin.
Christmas sets the centre at the edge.
And from this day our world is re-aligned;
A tiny seed unfolding in the womb
Becomes the source from which we all unfold
And flower into being. We are healed,
The End begins, the tomb becomes a womb,
For now in him all things are re-aligned.

3 Refugee

We think of him as safe beneath the steeple,
Or cosy in a crib beside the font,
But he is with a million displaced people
On the long road of weariness and want.
For even as we sing our final carol
His family is up and on that road,
Fleeing the wrath of someone else's quarrel,
Glancing behind and shouldering their load.
Whilst Herod rages still from his dark tower,
Christ clings to Mary, fingers tightly curled,
The lambs are slaughtered by the men of power,
And death squads spread their curse across the world.
But every Herod dies, and comes alone
To stand before the Lamb upon the throne.

St Stephen

Witness for Jesus, man of fruitful blood,
Your martyrdom begins and stands for all.
They saw the stones, you saw the face of God,
And sowed a seed that blossomed in St Paul.
When Saul departed breathing threats and slaughter,
He had to pass through that Damascus gate
Where he had held the coats and heard the laughter
As Christ, alive in you, forgave his hate,
And showed him the same light you saw from heaven
And taught him, through his blindness, how to see;
Christ did not ask, 'Why were you stoning Stephen?'
But, 'Saul, why are you persecuting me?'
Each martyr after you adds to his story,
As clouds of witness shine through clouds of glory.

New Year's Day: Church bells

Not the bleak speak of mobile messages,
The soft chime of synthesized reminders,
Not texts, not pagers, data packages,
Not satnav or locators ever find us
As surely, soundly, deeply as these bells
That sound and find and call us all at once.
'Ears of my ears' can hear, my body feels
This call to prayer that is itself a dance.
So ring them out in joy and jubilation,
Sound them in sorrow tolling for the lost,
O let them wake the Church and rouse the nation,
A sleeping lion stirred to life at last,
Begin again they sing, again begin,
A ring and rhythm answered from within.

EPIPHANY

1 The magi

It might have been just someone else's story;
Some chosen people get a special king,
We leave them to their own peculiar glory,
We don't belong, it doesn't mean a thing.
But when these three arrive they bring us with them,
Gentiles like us, their wisdom might be ours;
A steady step that finds an inner rhythm,
A pilgrim's eye that sees beyond the stars.
They did not know his name but still they sought him,
They came from otherwhere but still they found;
In palaces, found those who sold and bought him,
But in the filthy stable, hallowed ground.
Their courage gives our questing hearts a voice
To seek, to find, to worship, to rejoice.

2 The baptism of Christ

Beginning here we glimpse the Three-in-one;
The river runs, the clouds are torn apart,
The Father speaks, the Spirit and the Son
Reveal to us the single loving heart
That beats behind the being of all things
And calls and keeps and kindles us to light.
The dove descends, the spirit soars and sings,
'You are belovèd, you are my delight!'
In that swift light and life, as water spills
And streams around the Man like quickening rain,
The voice that made the universe reveals
The God in Man who makes it new again.
He calls us too, to step into that river,
To die and rise and live and love forever.

3 The call of the disciples

He calls us all to step aboard his ship,
Take the adventure on this morning's wing,
Raise sail with him, launch out into the deep,
Whatever storms or floods are threatening.
If faith gives way to doubt, or love to fear,
Then, as on Galilee, we'll rouse the Lord,
For he is always with us and will hear,
And make our peace with his creative Word,
Who made us, loved us, formed us and has set
All his beloved lovers in an ark;
Borne upwards by his Spirit, we will float
Above the rising waves, the falling dark,
As fellow pilgrims, driven towards that haven,
Where all will be redeemed, fulfilled, forgiven.

4 Nathanael

A fugitive and exile, Jacob slept,
A man of clay, his head upon a stone,
And even in his sleep his spirit wept,
He lay down lonely and would wake alone.
But in the night he dreamt the heavens parted
And glimpsed, in glory, as from heaven's core,
A ladder set for all the broken-hearted
And earth herself becoming heaven's door.
And when the nameless angel named him Israel
He kept this gift, whose depth he never knew;
The promise of an end to all our exile,
For now a child of Israel finds it true,
And sees the One who heals the deep heart's aching
As Jacob's dream becomes Nathanael's waking.

5 The miracle at Cana

Here's an epiphany to have and hold,
A truth that you can taste upon the tongue,
No distant shrines and canopies of gold
Or ladders to be clambered rung by rung,
But here and now, amidst your daily living,
Where you can taste and touch and feel and see,
The spring of love, the fount of all forgiving,
Flows when you need it, rich, abundant, free.
Better than waters of some outer weeping,
That leave you still with all your hidden sin,
Here is a vintage richer for the keeping
That works its transformation from within.
'What price?' you ask me, as we raise the glass,
'It cost our Saviour everything he has.'

St Paul

An enemy whom God has made a friend,
A righteous man discounting righteousness,
Last to believe and first for God to send,
He found the fountain in the wilderness.
Thrown to the ground and raised at the same moment,
A prisoner who set his captors free,
A naked man with love his only garment,
A blinded man who helped the world to see,
A Jew who had been perfect in the Law,
Blesses the flesh of every other race
And helps them see what the apostles saw –
The glory of the Lord in Jesus' face;
Strong in his weakness, joyful in his pains,
And bound by Love, who freed him from his chains.

Candlemas

They came, as called, according to the Law.
Though they were poor and had to keep things simple,
They moved in grace, in quietness, in awe,
For God was coming with them to his temple.
Amidst the outer court's commercial bustle
They'd waited hours, enduring shouts and shoves,
Buyers and sellers, sensing one more hustle,
Had made a killing on the two young doves.
They come at last with us to Candlemas
And keep the day the prophecies came true;
We share with them, amidst our busyness,
The peace that Simeon and Anna knew.
For Candlemas still keeps his kindled light:
Against the dark our Saviour's face is bright.

Ash Wednesday

Receive this cross of ash upon your brow,
Brought from the burning of Palm Sunday's cross;
The forests of the world are burning now
And you make late repentance for the loss.
But all the trees of God would clap their hands,
The very stones themselves would shout and sing,
If you could covenant to love these lands
And recognize in Christ their lord and king.
He sees the slow destruction of those trees,
He weeps to see the ancient places burn,
And still you make what purchases you please
And still to dust and ashes you return.
But hope could rise from ashes even now,
Beginning with this sign upon your brow.

TEMPTATIONS

1 Stones into bread

The Fountain thirsts, the Bread is hungry here,
The Light is dark, the Word without a voice.
When darkness speaks it seems so light and clear.
Now he must dare, with us, to make a choice.
In a distended belly's cruel curve
He feels the famine of the ones who lose,
He starves for those whom we have forced to starve,
He chooses now for those who cannot choose.
He is the staff and sustenance of life,
He lives for all from one sustaining Word,
His love still breaks and pierces like a knife
The stony ground of hearts that never shared,
God gives through him what Satan never could;
The broken bread that is our only food.

2 All the kingdoms of the world

'So here's the deal and this is what you get:
The penthouse suite with world-commanding views,
The banker's bonus and the private jet,
Control and ownership of all the news,
An "in" to that exclusive one percent,
Who know the score, who really run the show,
With interest on every penny lent
And sweeteners for cronies in the know.
A straight arrangement between me and you,
No hell below or heaven high above,
You just admit it, and give me my due
And wake up from this foolish dream of love . . .'
But Jesus laughed, 'You are not what you seem.
Love is the waking life, you are the dream.'

3 On the pinnacle

'Temples and spires are good for looking down from;
You stand above the world on holy heights,
Here on the pinnacle, above the maelstrom,
Among the few, the true, unearthly lights.
Here you can breathe the thin air of perfection
And feel your kinship with the lonely star,
Above the shadow and the pale reflection,
Here you can know for certain who you are.
The world is stalled below, but you could move it
If they could know you as you are up here.
Of course they'll doubt, but here's your chance to prove it!
Angels will bear you up, so have no fear . . .'
'I was not sent to look down from above,
It's fear that sets these tests and proofs, not love.'

Mothering Sunday

At last, in spite of all, a recognition
For those who loved and laboured for so long,
Who brought us, through that labour, to fruition,
To flourish in the place where we belong;
A thanks to those who stayed and did the raising,
Who buckled down and did the work of two,
Whom governments have mocked instead of praising,
Who hid their heart-break and still struggled through;
The single mothers forced on to the edge,
Whose work the world has overlooked, neglected,
Invisible to wealth and privilege,
But in whose lives the Kingdom is reflected.
Now into Christ our mother Church we bring them,
Who shares with them the birth-pangs of his Kingdom.

The Annunciation

We see so little, stayed on surfaces,
We calculate the outsides of all things,
Preoccupied with our own purposes
We miss the shimmer of the angels' wings.
They coruscate around us in their joy,
A swirl of wheels and eyes and wings unfurled;
They guard the good we purpose to destroy,
A hidden blaze of glory in God's world.
But on this day a young girl stopped to see
With open eyes and heart. She heard the voice –
The promise of his glory yet to be
As time stood still for her to make a choice.
Gabriel knelt and not a feather stirred.
The Word himself was waiting on her word.

HOLY WEEK

1 Palm Sunday

Now to the gate of my Jerusalem,
The seething holy city of my heart,
The Saviour comes. But will I welcome him?
Oh crowds of easy feelings make a start;
They raise their hands, get caught up in the singing,
And think the battle won. Too soon they'll find
The challenge, the reversal he is bringing
Changes their tune. I know what lies behind
The surface flourish that so quickly fades;
Self-interest, and fearful guardedness,
The hardness of the heart, its barricades,
And at the core, the dreadful emptiness
Of a perverted temple. Jesus, come
Break my resistance and make me your home.

2 Jesus weeps

Jesus comes near and he beholds the city
And looks on us with tears in his eyes,
And wells of mercy, streams of love and pity
Flow from the fountain whence all things arise.
He loved us into life and longs to gather
And meet with his beloved face to face.
How often has he called, a careful mother,
And wept for our refusals of his grace,
Wept for a world that, weary with its weeping,
Benumbed and stumbling, turns the other way;
Fatigued compassion is already sleeping
Whilst her worst nightmares stalk the light of day.
But we might waken yet, and face those fears,
If we could see ourselves through Jesus' tears.

3 Cleansing the Temple

Come to your Temple here with liberation
And overturn these tables of exchange,
Restore in me my lost imagination,
Begin in me for good the pure change.
Come as you came, an infant with your mother,
That innocence may cleanse and claim this ground.
Come as you came, a boy who sought his father
With questions asked and certain answers found.
Come as you came this day, a man in anger,
Unleash the lash that drives a pathway through,
Face down for me the fear, the shame, the danger,
Teach me again to whom my love is due.
Break down in me the barricades of death
And tear the veil in two with your last breath.

4 The anointing at Bethany

Come close with Mary, Martha, Lazarus,
So close the candles flare with their soft breath,
And kindle heart and soul to flame within us,
Lit by these mysteries of life and death.
For beauty now begins the final movement,
In quietness and intimate encounter,
The alabaster jar of precious ointment
Is broken open for the world's true lover.
The whole room richly fills to feast the senses
With all the yearning such a fragrance brings,
The heart is mourning but the spirit dances,
Here at the very centre of all things,
Here at the meeting place of love and loss
We all foresee and see beyond the cross.

5 Maundy Thursday

Here is the source of every sacrament,
The all-transforming presence of the Lord,
Replenishing our every element,
Remaking us in his creative Word.
For here the earth herself gives bread and wine,
The air delights to bear his Spirit's speech,
The fire dances where the candles shine,
The waters cleanse us with his gentle touch.
And here he shows the full extent of love
To us whose love is always incomplete,
In vain we search the heavens high above,
The God of love is kneeling at our feet.
Though we betray him, though it is the night,
He meets us here and loves us into light.

THE STATIONS OF THE CROSS

I Jesus is condemned to death

The very air that Pilate breathes, the voice
With which he speaks in judgement, all his powers
Of perception and discrimination, choice,
Decision, all his years, his days and hours,
His consciousness of self, his every sense,
Are given by this prisoner, freely given.
The man who stands there making no defence,
Is God. His hands are tied, his heart is open.
And he bears Pilate's heart in his and feels
That crushing weight of wasted life. He lifts
It up in silent love. He lifts and heals.
He gives himself again with all his gifts
Into our hands. As Pilate turns away
A door swings open. This is judgement day.

II Jesus is given his cross

He gives himself again with all his gifts
And now we give him something in return.
He gave the earth that bears, the air that lifts,
Water to cleanse and cool, fire to burn,
And from these elements he forged the iron,
From strands of life he wove the growing wood,
He made the stones that pave the roads of Zion,
He saw it all and saw that it is good.
We took his iron to edge an axe's blade,
We took the axe and laid it to the tree,
We made a cross of all that he has made,
And laid it on the one who made us free.
Now he receives again and lifts on high
The gifts he gave and we have turned awry.

III Jesus falls the first time

He made the stones that pave the roads of Zion
And well he knows the path we make him tread;
He met the devil as a roaring lion
And still refused to turn these stones to bread,
Choosing instead, as love will always choose,
This darker path into the heart of pain.
And now he falls upon the stones that bruise
The flesh, that break and scrape the tender skin.
He and the earth he made were never closer,
Divinity and dust come face to face.
We flinch back from his *via dolorosa*,
He sets his face like flint and takes our place,
Staggers beneath the black weight of us all
And falls with us that he might break our fall.

IV Jesus meets his mother

This darker path into the heart of pain
Was also hers whose love enfolded him
In flesh and wove him in her womb. Again
The sword is piercing. She, who cradled him
And gentled and protected her young son,
Must stand and watch the cruelty that mars
Her maiden making. Waves of pain that stun
And sicken pass across his face and hers
As their eyes meet. Now she enfolds the world
He loves in prayer; the mothers of the disappeared
Who know her pain, all bodies bowed and curled
In desperation on this road of tears,
All the grief-stricken in their last despair,
Are folded in the mantle of her prayer.

V Simon of Cyrene carries the cross

In desperation on this road of tears
Bystanders and bypassers turn away.
In other's pain we face our own worst fears
And turn our backs to keep those fears at bay,
Unless we are compelled as this man was
By force of arms or force of circumstance
To face and feel and carry someone's cross
In Love's full glare and not his backward glance.
So, Simon, no disciple, still fulfilled
The calling: 'Take the cross and follow me.'
By accident his life was stalled and stilled,
Becoming all he was compelled to be.
Make me, like him, your pressed man and your priest,
Your *alter Christus*, burdened and released.

VI Veronica wipes the face of Jesus

Bystanders and bypassers turn away
And wipe his image from their memory.
She keeps her station. She is here to stay
And stem the flow. She is the reliquary
Of his last look on her. The bloody sweat
And salt tears of his love are soaking through
The folds of her devotion and the wet
Folds of her handkerchief, like the dew
Of morning, like a softening rain of grace.
Because she wiped the grime from off his skin,
And glimpsed the godhead in his human face
Whose hidden image we all bear within,
Through all our veils and shrouds of daily pain
The face of God is shining once again.

VII Jesus falls the second time

Through all our veils and shrouds of daily pain,
Through our bruised bruises and re-opened scars,
He falls and stumbles with us, hurt again
When we are hurt again. With us he bears
The cruel repetitions of our cruelty;
The beatings of already beaten men,
The second rounds of torture, the futility
Of all unheeded pleading, every scream in vain.
And by this fall he finds the fallen souls
Who passed a first, but failed a second trial,
The souls who thought their faith would hold them whole
And found it only held them for a while.
Be with us when the road is twice as long
As we can bear. By weakness make us strong.

VIII Jesus meets the women of Jerusalem

He falls and stumbles with us, hurt again,
But still he holds the road and looks in love
On all of us who look on him. Our pain
As close to him as his. These women move
Compassion in him as he does in them.
He asks us both to weep and not to weep.
Women of Gaza and Jerusalem,
Women of every nation where the deep
Wounds of memory divide the land
And lives of all your children, where the mines
Of all our wars are sown: Afghanistan,
Iraq, the Cote d'Ivoire . . . he reads the signs
And weeps with you, and with you he will stay
Until the day he wipes your tears away.

IX Jesus falls the third time

He weeps with you and with you he will stay
When all your staying power has run out;
You can't go on, you go on anyway.
He stumbles just beside you when the doubt
That always haunts you cuts you down at last
And takes away the hope that drove you on.
This is the third fall and it hurts the worst,
This long descent through darkness to depression
From which there seems no rising and no will
To rise, or breathe or bear your own heartbeat.
Twice you survived; this third will surely kill,
And you could almost wish for that defeat
Except that in the cold hell where you freeze
You find your God beside you on his knees.

X Jesus is stripped of his garments

You can't go on, you go on anyway.
He goes with you, his cradle to your grave.
Now is the time to loosen, cast away
The useless weight of everything but love.
For he began his letting go before,
Before the worlds for which he dies were made,
Emptied himself, became one of the poor,
To make you rich in him and unafraid.
See, as they strip the robe from off his back
They strip away your own defences too,
Now you could lose it all and never lack,
Now you can see what naked love can do.
Let go these bonds beneath whose weight you bow,
His stripping strips you both for action now.

XI Crucifixion: Jesus is nailed to the cross

See, as they strip the robe from off his back
And spread his arms and nail them to the cross,
The dark nails pierce him and the sky turns black,
And love is firmly fastened on to loss.
But here a pure change happens. On this tree
Loss becomes gain, death opens into birth.
Here wounding heals and fastening makes free,
Earth breathes in heaven, heaven roots in earth.
And here we see the length, the breadth, the height,
Where love and hatred meet and love stays true,
Where sin meets grace and darkness turns to light,
We see what love can bear and be and do.
And here our Saviour calls us to his side,
His love is free, his arms are open wide.

XII Jesus dies on the cross

The dark nails pierce him and the sky turns black,
We watch him as he labours to draw breath.
He takes our breath away to give it back,
Return it to its birth through his slow death.
We hear him struggle, breathing through the pain,
Who once breathed out his spirit on the deep,
Who formed us when he mixed the dust with rain
And drew us into consciousness from sleep.
His Spirit and his life he breathes in all,
Mantles his world in his one atmosphere,
And now he comes to breathe beneath the pall
Of our pollutions, draw our injured air
To cleanse it and renew. His final breath
Breathes and bears us through the gates of death.

XIII Jesus' body is taken down from the cross

His spirit and his life he breathes in all,
Now on this cross his body breathes no more.
Here at the centre everything is still,
Spent, and emptied, opened to the core.
A quiet taking down, a prising loose,
A cross-beam lowered like a weighing scale,
Unmaking of each thing that had its use,
A long withdrawing of each bloodied nail.
This is ground zero, emptiness and space,
With nothing left to say or think or do,
But look unflinching on the sacred face
That cannot move or change or look at you.
Yet in that prising loose and letting be
He has unfastened you and set you free.

XIV Jesus is laid in the tomb

Here at the centre everything is still,
Before the stir and movement of our grief
That bears its pain with rhythm, ritual,
Beautiful useless gestures of relief.
So they anoint the skin that cannot feel
And soothe his ruined flesh with tender care,
Kissing the wounds they know they cannot heal,
With incense scenting only empty air.
He blesses every love that weeps and grieves,
And makes our grief the pangs of a new birth.
The love that's poured in silence at old graves,
Renewing flowers, tending the bare earth,
Is never lost. In him all love is found
And sown with him, a seed in the rich ground.

XV Easter dawn

He blesses every love that weeps and grieves
And now he blesses hers who stood and wept
And would not be consoled, or leave her love's
Last touching place, but watched as low light crept
Up from the east. A sound behind her stirs
A scatter of bright birdsong through the air.
She turns, but cannot focus through her tears,
Or recognize the Gardener standing there.
She hardly hears his gentle question, 'Why,
Why are you weeping?', or sees the play of light
That brightens as she chokes out her reply,
'They took my love away, my day is night.'
And then she hears her name, she hears Love say
The Word that turns her night, and ours, to Day.

Ascension Day

We saw his light break through the cloud of glory
Whilst we were rooted still in time and place,
As earth became a part of heaven's story
And heaven opened to his human face.
We saw him go and yet we were not parted,
He took us with him to the heart of things,
The heart that broke for all the broken-hearted
Is whole and heaven-centered now, and sings;
Sings in the strength that rises out of weakness,
Sings through the clouds that veil him from our sight,
Whilst we ourselves become his clouds of witness
And sing the waning darkness into light;
His light in us, and ours in him concealed,
Which all creation waits to see revealed.

The Visitation

Here is a meeting made of hidden joys,
Of lightenings cloistered in a narrow place,
From quiet hearts the sudden flame of praise
And in the womb the quickening kick of grace.
Two women on the very edge of things
Unnoticed and unknown to men of power,
But in their flesh the hidden Spirit sings
And in their lives the buds of blessing flower.
And Mary stands with all we call 'too young',
Elizabeth with all called 'past their prime'.
They sing today for all the great unsung,
Women who turned eternity to time,
Favoured of heaven, outcast on the earth,
Prophets who bring the best in us to birth.

Pentecost

Today we feel the wind beneath our wings,
Today the hidden fountain flows and plays,
Today the church draws breath at last and sings,
As every flame becomes a tongue of praise.
This is the feast of Fire, Air and Water,
Poured out and breathed and kindled into Earth.
The Earth herself awakens to her maker,
Translated out of death and into birth.
The right words come today in their right order
And every word spells freedom and release.
Today the gospel crosses every border,
All tongues are loosened by the Prince of Peace.
Today the lost are found in his translation,
Whose mother-tongue is love, in every nation.

Trinity Sunday

In the Beginning, not in time or space,
But in the quick before both space and time,
In Life, in Love, in co-inherent Grace,
In three in one and one in three, in rhyme,
In music, in the whole creation story,
In his own image, his imagination,
The Triune Poet makes us for his glory,
And makes us each the other's inspiration.
He calls us out of darkness, chaos, chance,
To improvise a music of our own,
To sing the chord that calls us to the dance,
Three notes resounding from a single tone,
To sing the End in whom we all begin;
Our God beyond, beside us, and within.

CORPUS CHRISTI

1 Love's choice

This bread is light, dissolving, almost air,
A little visitation on my tongue,
A wafer-thin sensation, hardly there.
This taste of wine is brief in flavour, flung
A moment to the palate's roof and fled,
Even its aftertaste a memory.
Yet this is how he comes. Through wine and bread
Love chooses to be emptied into me.
He does not come in unimagined light
Too bright to be denied, too absolute
For consciousness, too strong for sight,
Leaving the seer blind, the poet mute;
Chooses instead to seep into each sense,
To dye himself into experience.

2 Hide and seek

Ready or not, you tell me, *here I come!*
And so I know I'm hiding, and I know
My hiding place is useless. You will come
And find me. You are searching high and low.
Today I'm hiding low, down here, below,
Below the sunlit surface others see.
Oh find me quickly, quickly come to me.
And here you come and here I come to you.
I come to you because you come to me.
You know my hiding places. I know you,
I reach you through your hiding places too;
Feeling for the thread, but now I see –
Even in darkness I can see you shine,
Risen in bread, and revelling in wine.

ST JOHN THE BAPTIST

1 St John's eve

Midsummer night, and bonfires on the hill
Burn for the man who makes way for the Light:
'He must increase and I diminish still,
Until his sun illuminates my night.'
So John the Baptist pioneers our path,
Unfolds the essence of the life of prayer,
Unlatches the last doorway into faith,
And makes one inner space an everywhere.
Least of the new and greatest of the old,
Orpheus on the threshold with his lyre,
He sets himself aside, and cries, 'Behold
The One who stands amongst you comes with fire!'
So keep his fires burning through this night,
Beacons and gateways for the child of light.

2 Baptism

Love's hidden thread has drawn us to the font,
A wide womb floating on the breath of God,
Feathered with seraph wings, lit with the swift
Lightening of praise, with thunder over-spread,
And under-girded with an unheard song,
Calling through water, fire, darkness, pain,
Calling us to the life for which we long,
Yearning to bring us to our birth again.
Again the breath of God is on the waters
In whose reflecting face our candles shine,
Again he draws from death the sons and daughters
For whom he bid the elements combine.
As living stones around a font today,
Rejoice with those who roll the stone away.

St Peter

Impulsive master of misunderstanding,
You comfort me with all your big mistakes;
Jumping the ship before you make the landing,
Placing the bet before you know the stakes.
I love the way you step out without knowing,
The way you sometimes speak before you think,
The way your broken faith is always growing,
The way he holds you even when you sink.
Born to a world that always tried to shame you,
Your shaky ego vulnerable to shame,
I love the way that Jesus chose to name you,
Before you knew how to deserve that name.
And in the end your Saviour let you prove
That each denial is undone by love.

St Thomas the Apostle

'We do not know . . . how can we know the way?'
Courageous master of the awkward question,
You spoke the words the others dared not say
And cut through their evasion and abstraction.
O doubting Thomas, father of my faith,
You put your finger on the nub of things:
We cannot love some disembodied wraith,
But flesh and blood must be our king of kings.
Your teaching is to touch, embrace, anoint,
Feel after him and find him in the flesh.
Because he loved your awkward counterpoint,
The Word has heard and granted you your wish.
O place my hands with yours, help me divine
The wounded God whose wounds are healing mine.

St Mary Magdalene

Men called you light so as to load you down,
And burden you with their own weight of sin,
A woman forced to cover and contain
Those seven devils sent by Everyman.
But one man set you free and took your part,
One man knew and loved you to the core.
The broken alabaster of your heart
Revealed to him alone a hidden door,
Into a garden where the fountain sealed,
Could flow at last for him in healing tears,
Till, in another garden, he revealed
The perfect love that cast out all your fears,
And quickened you with love's own sway and swing,
As light and lovely as the news you bring.

Transfiguration

For that one moment, in and out of time,
On that one mountain where all moments meet,
The daily veil that covers the sublime
In darkling glass fell dazzled at his feet.
There were no angels full of eyes and wings,
Just living glory full of truth and grace.
The love that dances at the heart of things
Shone out upon us from a human face.
And to that light the light in us leaped up,
We felt it quicken somewhere deep within,
A sudden blaze of long-extinguished hope
Trembled and tingled through the tender skin.
Nor can this blackened sky, this darkened scar,
Eclipse that glimpse of how things really are.

St Michael and All Angels

Michaelmas gales assail the waning year,
And Michael's scale is true, his blade is bright.
He strips dead leaves, and leaves the living clear
To flourish in the touch and reach of light.
Archangel bring your balance, help me turn
Upon this turning world with you and dance
In the Great Dance. Draw near, help me discern,
And trace the hidden grace in change and chance.
Angel of fire, love's fierce radiance,
Drive through the deep until the steep waves part;
Undo the dragon's sinuous influence
And pierce the clotted darkness in my heart.
Unchain the child you find there, break the spell
And overthrow the tyrannies of hell.

ALL SAINTS

1 The gathered glories

Though Satan breaks our dark glass into shards,
Each shard still shines with Christ's reflected light,
It glances from the eyes, kindles the words
Of all his unknown saints. The dark is bright
With quiet lives and steady lights undimmed,
The witness of the ones we shunned and shamed.
Plain in our sight and far beyond our seeing,
He weaves their threads into the web of being.
They stand beside us even as we grieve,
The lone and left behind whom no one claimed,
Unnumbered multitudes, he lifts above
The shadow of the gibbet and the grave,
To triumph where all saints are known and named;
The gathered glories of his wounded love.

2 A last beatitude

And blessèd are the ones we overlook;
The faithful servers on the coffee rota,
The ones who hold no candle, bell or book
But keep the books and tally up the quota,
The gentle souls who come to 'do the flowers',
The quiet ones who organize the fete,
Church sitters who give up their weekday hours,
Doorkeepers who may open heaven's gate.
God knows the depths that often go unspoken
Amongst the shy, the quiet, and the kind,
Or the slow healing of a heart long broken,
Placing each flower so for a year's mind.
Invisible on earth, without a voice,
In heaven their angels glory and rejoice.

3 Thanksgiving

Thanksgiving starts with thanks for mere survival,
Just to have made it through another year
With everyone still breathing. But we share
So much beyond the outer roads we travel;
Our interweavings on a deeper level,
The modes of life embodied souls can share,
The unguessed blessings of our being here,
Threads of connection no one can unravel.
So I give thanks for our deep coinherence,
Inwoven in the web of God's own grace,
Pulling us through the grave and gate of death.
I thank him for the truth behind appearance,
I thank him for his light in every face,
I thank him for us all, with every breath.

Remembrance Sunday

November pierces with its bleak remembrance
Of all the bitterness and waste of war;
Our silence tries but fails to make a semblance
Of that lost peace they thought worth fighting for,
Our silence seethes instead with wraiths and whispers
And all the restless rumour of new wars,
For shells are falling all around our vespers,
No moment is unscarred, there is no pause.
In every instant bloodied innocence
Falls to the weary earth, and whilst we stand
Quiescence ends again in acquiescence,
And Abel's blood still cries from every land.
One silence only might redeem that blood;
Only the silence of a dying God.

The Feast of Christ the King

Our King is calling from the hungry furrows
Whilst we are cruising through the aisles of plenty,
Our hoardings screen us from the man of sorrows,
Our soundtracks drown his murmur: 'I am thirsty.'
He stands in line to sign in as a stranger
And seek a welcome from the world he made,
We see him only as a threat, a danger,
He asks for clothes, we strip-search him instead.
And if he should fall sick then we take care
That he does not infect our private health,
We lock him in the prisons of our fear
Lest he unlock the prison of our wealth.
But still on Sunday we shall stand and sing
The praises of our hidden Lord and King.

Epilogue: Sanctus

We gather as his Church on God's good earth
And listen to the Requiem's intense,
Long, love-laden keening, calling forth
Echoes of Eden, blessing every sense
With brimming blisses, every death with birth,
Until all passion passes into praise.
I bless the hidden threads that drew us here,
I bless this day, distinct amidst our days,
I bless the light, the music-laden air,
I bless the interweaving of our ways,
The lifting of the burdens that we bear,
I bless the broken body that we share.
Sanctus the heart, *Sanctus* the spirit cries,
Sanctus the flesh in every touch replies.

Appendix A

The seven 'Great O' Antiphons in their Latin and English texts

O Sapientia, quae ex ore Altissimi prodiisti,
attingens a fine usque ad finem,
fortiter suaviterque disponens omnia:
veni ad docendum nos viam prudentiae.

O Wisdom, coming forth from the mouth of the Most High,
reaching from one end to the other mightily,
and sweetly ordering all things:
Come and teach us the way of prudence.

O Adonai, et Dux domus Israel,
qui Moysi in igne flammae rubi apparuisti,
et ei in Sina legem dedisti:
veni ad redimendum nos in brachio extento.

O Adonai, and leader of the House of Israel,
who appeared to Moses in the fire of the burning bush
and gave him the law on Sinai:
Come and redeem us with an outstretched arm.

O Radix Jesse, qui stas in signum populorum,
super quem continebunt reges os suum,
quem Gentes deprecabuntur:
veni ad liberandum nos, jam noli tardare.

O Root of Jesse, standing as a sign among the peoples;
before you kings will shut their mouths,
to you the nations will make their prayer:
Come and deliver us, and delay no longer.

O Clavis David, et sceptrum domus Israel;
qui aperis, et nemo claudit;
claudis, et nemo aperit:
veni, et educ vinctum de domo carceris,
sedentem in tenebris, et umbra mortis.

O Key of David and sceptre of the House of Israel;
you open and no one can shut;
you shut and no one can open:
Come and lead the prisoners from the prison house,
those who dwell in darkness and the shadow of death.

O Oriens, splendor lucis aeternae,
et sol justitiae:
veni, et illumina sedentes
in tenebris, et umbra mortis.

O Dayspring,
splendour of light eternal and sun of righteousness:
Come and enlighten those who dwell in darkness
and the shadow of death.

O Rex Gentium, et desideratus earum,
lapisque angularis, qui facis utraque unum:
veni, et salva hominem,
quem de limo formasti.

O King of the nations, and their desire,
the cornerstone making both one:
Come and save the human race,
which you fashioned from clay.

O Emmanuel, Rex et legifer noster,
exspectatio Gentium, et Salvator earum:
veni ad salvandum nos, Domine, Deus noster.

O Emmanuel, our king and our lawgiver,
the hope of the nations and their Saviour:
Come and save us, O Lord our God.

Appendix B

The sonnets and liturgy

FRASER WATTS

There is an ancient tradition of having readings, other than from scripture, in Christian worship, even though it is probably a minority of churches that are currently maintaining that ancient tradition. The practice of including non-scriptural readings in lectionaries goes back as far as lectionaries themselves. In recounting this history, A. C. Bouquet draws attention to St Jerome's comment that other books were read 'for example of life and instruction of manners', and to Gregory the Great's comment that 'homilies of the Fathers were read at matins, and the biographies of the saints on their festivals' (Bouquet, 1939). The Eastern Orthodox Church created the 'Philokalia', a collection of readings from spiritual masters for the use of monks. It seems that, in an early draft of the lectionary for Book of Common Prayer, Cranmer included readings from the lives of the saints, to be read on their festivals, but later decided on an entirely biblical selection of readings.

Various purposes can be served by the use of non-scriptural readings. They can be informative, an aide to reflection and deeper understanding, an aide to devotion and spiritual practice, a source of advice about practical living, and so on. Simply allowing non-scriptural readings creates an atmosphere of freedom in exploration of the faith that many will find helpful. It also forges links between Christianity and contemporary culture, something that is very helpful in our present missionary situation.

For those open in principle to non-scriptural readings, a rich range of resources is potentially available, but poetry is one of the most valuable of these. Several anthologies of poetry linked to scripture are available (for example, Atwan and Weider, 1993; Atwan et al., 1998), and there are some poetry sequences linked to scripture (such as Sansom, 1956). There are also several more varied volumes of religious or Christian verse (for example, Bailey, 1983; Batchelor, 1995; Causley, 1982; Davie, 1981; Gardner, 1972; Gregory and Zaturenska, 1957; Levi, 1984; Nicholson, 1942). There are also anthologies for the church year that include a varied mixture of prose, prayer and poetry (for example, Every et al., 1990; Richards, 1998; Hebblethwaite, 2000).

The most common way to use poetry in church services is to use one poem in the service, alongside the scripture readings. The poem can be linked directly to one of the scripture readings, serving as a commentary on it. Alternatively, it can be linked to the general theme of the service, or (as here) to that day in the church year. I know of no other book that offers a set of poems for the church year in the way that Malcolm Guite has done here. As priest and liturgist of the church for which they have been written, St Edward's Church in central Cambridge to which Malcolm Guite and I both belong, I can testify to how much they have enriched our worship.

The use of poetry in services perhaps works best where there is a clear theme to the service, to which the poem can relate. I very much regret the fact that in 2000 the Church of England abandoned an authorized thematic lectionary, though thematic services are still possible under the general provision for Services of the Word. Reading books of the Bible continuously over a number of Sundays seems to disregard the fact that a growing proportion of church attenders are unable to come every Sunday, and that even those who come regularly are unlikely to remember last Sunday's readings clearly enough to form any real linkage in the mind.

The reality is that, unless a church service coheres within itself, coherence is lost altogether in the minds of churchgoers. On the other hand, within a coherent, thematic service, a poem related to the theme, or to the day in the Church year, makes a powerful contribution. Where a poem relates specifically to one of the Bible readings, it obviously comes best immediately after that reading. Where the poem relates to the theme more generally, there is more flexibility about where it comes in the sequence of readings. At St Edward's, we tend to place the sonnet either first or last in the sequence.

In a Eucharist, there is seldom space for more than one sonnet. However, in a non-Eucharistic service there is scope for using a sonnet sequence to provide the core of the service. There are several sequences of sonnets in this collection that lend themselves to being used in this way, and I will illustrate the point with three sequences: Advent, Epiphany and the Stations of the Cross.

The Promise of His Glory (pp. 114–16) suggests an interesting way of using the Advent antiphons, in which all seven antiphons are used sequentially in a single service, and each is followed by a short Bible reading and the appropriate verse of the hymn, 'O Come, O Come, Emmanuel', which is itself based on the Advent antiphons. At St Edward's, we have been using a version of this for some years. In fact we have tried doing it in two different ways.

On Advent Sunday we often begin our 5.00 p.m. service with a candlelit procession, singing the antiphons at different stations in the church, each followed by a Bible reading. A verse of the hymn is then sung as we move on to the next station. Often we have just used the five antiphons, which have corresponding verses in the hymn-book version of 'O Come, O Come, Emmanuel'. The procession moves from west to east, singing the antiphons at different stations: 'O Key of David' at the west door, 'O King of the nations' at the font, 'O Wisdom' at the lectern, 'O Dayspring' at the advent candle, and 'O Emmanuel' at the sanctuary. Inspired by this liturgy, Malcolm Guite wrote a sonnet for each of the antiphons.

We have also used all seven antiphons at a Sunday morning Service of the Word. For each antiphon we first hear the scripture reading on which it is based, then listen to the plainsong antiphon itself, then hear the sonnet based on the antiphon, and finally allow silence to fall before moving on to the next antiphon. After all seven antiphons, the whole congregation sings 'O Come, O Come, Emmanuel'. It creates a different atmosphere doing this without procession, one that is cool, still and contemplative.

The sequence of Epiphany sonnets also provides a good basis for a Service of the Word. Again, there is a helpful basis in 'A Service for the Feast of the Baptism of the Lord' in *The Promise of his Glory*, pp. 210–22. The service moves through three core Gospel readings for the Feast of the Epiphany, the coming of the Magi, the first miracle at Cana, and the baptism of Jesus. This collection provides a sonnet for each of these Gospel readings. The service can be expanded to include the calling of the first disciples, another core Epiphany Gospel for which there is also a sonnet in this collection.

In Holy Week there are sonnets for each day, meditating on the cleansing of the temple, the anointing at Bethany, and so forth, which we have incorporated into brief meditative services for those weekday evenings. Then, as a distinct set, there are sonnets for the Stations of the Cross.

Journeying with Jesus through the 'stations' (or stopping places) of the cross has its origins in the desire of pilgrims to the Holy Land to follow literally in the footsteps of Jesus. But not everyone could be there physically, and it was the Franciscans in the Middle Ages who had the idea of setting up a series of 'stations' to walk with Christ, in any church or public street, or even in people's own imagination. The stations take us on a journey from the judgement hall of Pilate, through various encounters along the road to the crucifixion itself, the taking down and the burial; sometimes a fifteenth station is added for the Resurrection. Each of these stations is a rich iconic source for reflection, and many of them are beautifully represented in art.

Churches that have the stations around their walls can obviously use the sonnets in a sequence as people move round the church. However, they can be used in many other ways. A thematic selection of them can be used, focusing for example on Jesus' solitary struggle with his cross, or on the people with whom he interacted on the way to Golgotha. At St Edward's, we built a Service of the Word for Passion Sunday, focusing on the stations in which Jesus interacted with others, each of whom can represent some aspect of ourselves. We used the remaining sonnets at the three-hour service on Good Friday.

It is best if the stations are presented fairly directly, in some way or other, before the sonnets reflecting on them are used (especially for a congregation not familiar with them). If there are no stations around the church, artistic representations can be projected on to a screen. Alternatively, narrative prose material can be used before each sonnet, and at St Edward's we used short extracts from *Walking the Way of Sorrows*, by K. K. Whitley (1989).

It is also helpful to include the congregation liturgically in each station. A short prayer or collect can be used after each sonnet. Psalms can also work well with the stations of the cross, especially psalms of lament. At St Edward's, we use Psalms 69, 130 and 137, and the canticle, 'O Saviour of the World'.

It is in the nature of poetry that it speaks to the heart as well as the head. Sonnets such as these fall fresh on the ears, enrich and deepen understanding, and open up new resonances. Liturgy serves various functions, but I believe the Church needs to be more aware of the potential of liturgy to contribute to Christian transformation, and to construct liturgy in a way that assists with that transformation. Our experience in using these sonnets at St Edward's over several years is that liturgy that is enriched through the use of sonnets does indeed help to change people. It also enables liturgy to connect with a broader range of people and so, perhaps surprisingly, contributes towards Church growth. There is a widespread hunger in our society for spiritual depth, and sonnets such as these help the Church to meet that need.

Bibliography

Robert Atwan and Laurence Wieder, 1993, *Chapters into Verse, Volume I: Genesis to Malachi*, Oxford: Oxford University Press.

Robert Atwan and Laurence Wieder, 1993, *Chapters into Verse, Volume II: Gospels to Revelations*, Oxford: Oxford University Press.

Robert Atwan, George Dardess and Peggy Rosenthal (eds), 1998, *Divine Inspiration: The Life of Jesus in World Poetry*, Oxford: Oxford University Press.

Gordon Bailey (ed.), 1983, *100 Contemporary Christian Poets*, Tring: Lion Publishing.

Mary Batchelor (ed.), 1995, *The Lion Christian Poetry Collection*, Oxford: Lion Publishing.

A. C. Bouquet, 1949, *A Lectionary of Christian Prose: From the 2nd to the 20th Century*, London: Longmans, Green & Co.

Charles Causley (ed.), 1982, *The Sun, Dancing: Christian Verse*, Harmondsworth: Puffin.

Church of England, 1990, *The Promise of His Glory: Services and Prayers for the Season from All Saints to Candlemas*, London: Church House Publishing and Mowbray.

Donald Davie (ed.), 1981, *The New Oxford Book of Christian Verse*, Oxford: Oxford University Press.

George Every, Richard Harries and Kallistos Ware (eds), 1990, *Seasons of the Spirit*, London: Triangle.

Helen Gardner (ed.), 1972, *The Faber Book of Religious Verse*, London: Faber & Faber.

Horace Gregory and Marya Zaturenska (eds), 1957, *The Mentor Book of Religious Verse*, New York: The New American Library.

Margaret Hebblethwaite (ed.), 2000, *The Living Spirit: Prayers and Readings for the Christian Year*, Norwich: Canterbury Press.

Peter Levi (ed.), 1984, *The Penguin Book of English Christian Verse*, Harmondsworth: Penguin.

Norman Nicholson (ed.), 1942, *An Anthology of Religious Verse: Designed for the Times*, Harmondsworth: Penguin.

H. J. Richards, 1998, *An Anthology for the Church Year*, Bury St Edmunds: Kevin Mayhew.

Clive Sansom, 1956, *The Witnesses*, London: Methuen.

Katerina Katsarka Whitley, 1989, *Walking the Way of Sorrows: Stations of the Cross*, Harrisburg, PA: Morehouse Publishing.

Index of Scriptural References

Gospel according to St Mark

Gospel according to St Luke

Gospel according to St John

Index of Liturgical Seasons

Since the book itself is broadly arranged by season, this index indicates only poems appropriate to specific days within those seasons and then other important but non-seasonal feast days (UK, US, Canada) in a separate list at the end.

Good Friday Stations I–XIV pp37–43
Holy Saturday Stations XIV, Jesus is laid in the tomb p43
Easter Day Stations XV, Easter dawn p44; St Thomas the Apostle p54;
　　Mary Magdalene p55

Specific days in Easter
St Mark Mark p4; The lectern p2
Ascension Ascension Day p45
The Visitation The Visitation p46
Pentecost Pentecost p47

Specific days in Season after Pentecost
St Matthew Matthew p3; The lectern p2
St Luke Luke p5; The lectern p2
Trinity Sunday Trinity Sunday p48; The baptism of Christ p20
Corpus Christi Love's choice p49; Hide and seek p50; John p6; Stones
　　into bread p27
The Nativity of St John the Baptist St John's eve p51; Baptism p52;
　　The Visitation p46; The baptism of Christ p20
Sts Peter and Paul, Apostles St Peter p53; St Paul p24
St Thomas St Thomas the Apostle p54
St Mary Magdalene St Mary Magdalene p55; Stations XV, Easter
　　dawn p44; The anointing at Bethany p35
St Mary the Virgin Mary p14; The Annunciation p31; Stations IV,
　　Jesus meets his mother p38; Luke 5
Transfiguration Transfiguration p56
Holy Cross Day Stations II, Jesus is given his cross p37; Stations V,
　　Simon of Cyrene carries the cross p39; Stations XI, Crucifixion,
　　Jesus is nailed to the cross p42
St Michael and All Angels St Michael and All Angels p57
All Saints The gathered glories p58; A last beatitude p59;
　　Thanksgiving p60
The Feast of Christ the King The Feast of Christ the King p62; O Rex
　　Gentium p12

Other Important Days
Mother's Day (US) Mothering Sunday p30
Memorial Day (US) Remembrance Sunday p61
Independence Day (US) Church bells p18
Reformation Sunday The lectern p2; Matthew p3; Mark p4; Luke p5;
　　John p6
Remembrance Day Remembrance Sunday p61
Thanksgiving Day (US and Canada) Thanksgiving p60
Any Saint The call of the disciples p21